P9-CTO-994

Visiting Her in Queens Is More Enlightening than a Month in a Monastery in Tibet

poems by
Michael Mark

Rattle | *Studio City, California* | 2022

*Visiting Her in Queens Is More Enlightening
than a Month in a Monastery in Tibet*
Copyright © 2022 by Michael Mark

All rights reserved

Layout and design by Timothy Green

Photographs:
Cover and pages 21–22 by Michael Mark
Back cover by Lois Alter Mark
Page 37 by Alan Mark

ISBN: 978-1-931307-51-2

First edition

Rattle Foundation
12411 Ventura Blvd
Studio City, CA 91604
www.rattle.com

The Rattle Foundation is an independent 501(c)3 non-profit, whose mission is to promote the practice of poetry, and which is not affiliated with any other organization. All poems are works of the imagination. While the perceptions and insights are based on the author's experience, no reference to any real person is intended or should be inferred.

CONTENTS

ACKNOWLEDGMENTS

I am thankful to all the people who helped me with my poetry, and to the editors of the following publications where some of these poems first appeared. And, of course, my patient, inspiring, loving family.

Alaska Quarterly Review: "Estelle"

Dunes Review: "Dad, Leave Mom"

Grist: A Journal of the Literary Arts: "Watching the Golden Gate Bridge Disappear"

I-70 Review: "My Mother's Disease Prays to the Same God as My Mother"

The Lascaux Review: "Spoiled"

Michigan Quarterly Review: "The Year We're Living In" and "It's All in Your Head, Estelle"

Pleiades: "Souvenirs"

Poetry East: "Nothing's as Hard as We Make It"

Portland Review: "She Fools Me Every Time"

Rattle: "First Date" and "A Daily Practice"

Santa Fe Literary Review: "Portrait in Alzheimer's Disease"

The Southern Review: "The Wish," "What My Father Heard the Rabbi Say at My Mother's Funeral," and "Celebrating His 92nd Birthday the Year His Wife Dies"

Sugar House Review: "If I Say, The Butterfly Is Beautiful, Dad"

The Sun: "What Are the Odds," "Dancing with My Father at My Son's Wedding," "Estelle and Bob," and "Visiting Her in Queens Is More Enlightening than a Month in a Monastery in Tibet"

Zocalo Public Square: "Losing My Parents in a Small CVS Drug Store"

Visiting Her in Queens Is More Enlightening than a Month in a Monastery in Tibet

Estelle

Even when they danced, Dad couldn't keep her
in his arms. She'd spin off, leave him to fade

back into the circle of others, clapping, hooting.
Days when the pond would freeze, mothers took

their children's hands and worried them around
in slow circles. Mom raced in unchartable loops

past me and my brother like we weren't hers.
Same way she didn't see my report card Fs as Fs.

She'd take the matching color pen and glide
the ballpoint so it looked like the B was always there.

You could ask how she convinced the butcher
that his scale was wrong, how she'd roll her cart away

with three-eighths of a pound of corned beef, paying
for only a quarter—fat trimmed, the way dad liked—

but she'd skim that question like she did all surfaces,
even air. Now she's given her own memory the slip.

Doctors say there's no reaching her.

The Year We're Living In

He's the breakfast cook. Half
grapefruit, half cup of coffee each;
they split a piece of toast. Mid-mornings,

I sit with her while he sleeps
in his glasses, exhausted from the all-
night watch. She's a wanderer.

Wednesdays and Fridays, when he plays
poker, she likes me to lie beside her.
If she calls me his name, I nod.

When it's the three of us, I'll say,
I'm Michael—your son!
She laughs, *I know!*

She does and she doesn't,
the neurologist says, depending
on the moment, the year she's living in.

Where are we going? she asks
from my old spot in back. I'm the driver now.
Wendy's, he says, *chicken nuggets.*

Burger King! She screams. *Hamburger!*
He reminds her, *Estelle, you don't like hamburgers. Wendy's
is your favorite!*

She calls him: *mean, stupid, murderer.*
I lower my window, then hers, his, turn
the radio all the way up and drive slow.

I don't know where we're going.

My Mother's Disease Prays to the Same God as My Mother

She's singing and cleaning the oven again.
Scrubbing with detergents and steel wool without
the rubber gloves to protect her sores.

My father slides a chair to watch.
She calls him God, maybe because he's always
telling her what to do.

He reminds her to unplug the can opener before
she washes it, the toaster oven, too, and the Mr. Coffee
that's been warming two cups of decaf

since midnight. She spreads the used ammonia-soaked rags
over the burners to dry. He moves them
to the window, opens it a little more, checks

that the car is still out there. When she asks,
"Is it good enough?" he says, "Yes."
From the gold-flecked linoleum, she calls him closer.

"Look what I have done for you, God."
He could make a joke—God can see from anywhere—
but he gets up, bends as low as she needs

to believe he's judging her work, maybe her soul.
"Good," he says.
And of course he knows, because you don't

have to be God to know, she'll put her head
right back in the oven—her whole body could fit now,
she's that tiny. She'll start cleaning again

[...]

and singing, part Yiddish, part gibberish, echoing
in the metal cave. What else can God do
but tap his brown-socked foot.

Sparrow

What did you eat today, Mom?
She says tuna.

The correct answer is crust from a lemon
pound cake she shredded with her chewed fingers
then puzzled together.

Is it night or day, Mom?

The window shades are pulled. People look
in, she thinks. Sometimes she peeks
from a corner to tell me. Not today.

How old are you, Mom?

What's this color?

I steady her on the bathroom scale.
What do you think you weigh, Mom?
Like a bird, she answers.

79 pounds.

I tuck her clothes but there's nothing
to hold onto. She cries the belt is breaking her;
she sticks herself undoing the safety pins.

What's smaller than extra small?
This question's meant for me.

Like a bird, she answers.

It's All in Your Head, Estelle

All she wants to do now is kiss, my Dad tells me
when I come for Mom's 90th. *That's nice,*
I say. *It's sad,* he whispers. This is also new:
my hair-trigger father is a famous shouter. Blames
the printing press for numbing his hearing.
Hers is sharper than ever. *She thinks everyone's
talking about her.* I nod. I've seen her try to listen
through walls, stand in corners, thin as a lamp.
I lean closer, calibrate a whisper loud enough
for him to hear, hushed so she doesn't: *That's
the disease.* He puts his palm over my mouth,
points to the hallway. A shadow. *Thing is,*
he says so low I can hardly hear, *she's right.
But she begs me to tell her it's all in her head.
So I do. It's crazy.* Crazy is what the whole block
called Jeffrey Dorn. He peeled paint off walls
and ate it. His parents sent him away.
She shuffles around the corner in her slippers
and nightgown—all she wears. Stops
in front of him. Pulls his face to her puckered lips.

What Are the Odds

That this trip isn't the stupidest thing he'll ever do

That they won't drive one mile before she asks, *Where are we going?* three times

That she'll ask why can't she drive anymore

That she'll cry her teeth hurt, she doesn't want to go, where's her momma

That she'll ask if she's dying

That she'll ask if he's dying

That she'll say he's not driving to the casino; he's putting her in a home

That the handicap spot will be open in front of the lobby

That the manager will accept his expired voucher for two free nights and throw
in two coupons for a free buffet

That he'll hit a blackjack

That she'll agree to stay at her slot machine until he comes back for her
but will get up, get lost, and scream until security comes

That she'll remember their room number

That she'll look at her arm where he will have written the room number

That he'll be able to play the required three hours a day to earn the free room

That he'll be able to concentrate and not make dumb bets like last time

That she'll leave her purse in the ladies' room, or the car, the buffet, the
coffee shop

That they'll find her purse each time

That it will still contain her wallet, which he will empty except for $10 and
a copy of her license

That she'll remember to stay in the room when she wakes up from her nap

That he'll remember to tape WE ARE IN ATLANTIC CITY to the back of
the door

That she'll remember not to double-lock the door because then he'll have to get
security to open it

That they'll split a muffin and cup of coffee every morning

That they'll find a sunny bench on the boardwalk

That he won't yell at her when she tries to take home the hotel ice bucket

That this will be the last time in Atlantic City

That they'll come home winners

Souvenirs

My mother takes the robe
from the hotel closet and the hangers.
Then looks out the window

and points: *See? You forget!*
She takes the Atlantic Ocean, folds
it over several times to fit

into my suitcase. *And what about these?*
She picks the thousands of roses
from the carpet. *And this?*—

slips the painting of the beach ball
and child from the wall. After telling her
these are not mine,

what can I say to the woman
who tells everyone I am the reason
for the flowers and the rain, and

the sun revolves around me, but
Sorry, Mom, next time I'll remember. She takes
the box of tissues, sweeps

every grain of sand off the beach,
collects the small shampoos, the plastic cups,
the coffee maker, all the bed linens and,

though I remind her we always
have the sun, she finds
enough room for the table lamp.

Portrait in Alzheimer's Disease

It's like she left and came back with a new haircut

left and came back with a scar

left and came back with different eyes, not

the eyes everyone said we shared

but the scar was gone

and she spoke a strange language and

left and came back without a son and

left and came back and never came back

Visiting Her in Queens Is More Enlightening than a Month in a Monastery in Tibet

For the fourth time my mother
asks, "How many children
do you have?" I'm beginning

to believe my answer,
"Two, Mom," is wrong. Maybe
the lesson is they are not mine,

not owned by me, and
she is teaching me about
my relationship with her.

I wash my dish and hers.
She washes them again. I ask why.
She asks why I care.

Before bed she unlocks and opens
the front door. While she sleeps
I close and lock it. She gets up. Unlocks it.

"What I have no one wants," she says.
I nod. She nods.
Are we agreeing?

My shrunken guru says she was up all night
preparing a salad for my breakfast.
She serves me an onion.

I want her to make French toast
for me like she used to.
I want to tell her about my pain,

and I want her to make it go away.
I want the present to be as good as
the past she does not remember.

I toast white bread for her, butter it,
cut it in half. I eat a piece of onion.
She asks me why I'm crying.

Losing My Parents in a Small CVS Drug Store

A woman who looks as old as them says try by the toilet paper.
My parents might be the ones stooped over, calculating the price
per quilted sheet.

An employee with an I CARE button saw them in Greeting Cards,
reading to each other, "To The Best Uncle," "For The Special Bride," "Our
Sincere Condolences," "Congratulations Graduate!"

A man with a backpack noticed them at the adult diapers, bewildered
by the poster's question, Are You Chafing? He overheard my mother
ask my father, "Are *you*?" My father asked back, "Are *you*?"

The stock boy caught them in the Employees Only restroom, admiring
the hand soap and the bathroom spray, Hawaiian Calm.

The surveillance camera shows them struggling between Twizzlers,
Peppermint Patties and the dietetic peanut butter clusters. By the time
I get there, just empty wrappers—so I have the manager

make an announcement, "Attention Michael's parents—please report
to checkout immediately without rushing too much. Your son trusts you
and wants you to have your independence but he doesn't want you to miss
Jeopardy." He adds, "And please remember our annual sale on tweezers
and double-soft Q-tips."

They move up from Deodorants and Toothpaste in slow motion. Each pushes
a cart for stability. Store workers cheer. Customers clear a path for their carts—
empty except for his Mrs. Potato Head and her Mister, for which they have
a two-for-one coupon.

"Did you find everything?" the cashier asks. "Did we?" my father asks my mother.
My mother asks back, "Did we?"

Dad, Leave Mom

while she sleeps. Tape *I'll be back* on the bathroom mirror, the trash can, under the carpet's corner, where you can't believe anyone in their right mind would ever look. Take the keys—house, car, garage, mailbox. Take a red-eye from JFK—business class—*never in a million years*, I know, still. Fly past the twice a day horse pill moon, cheese sandwich cut in half moon, pee stained sheets moon, doctor's blank face moon. Nurse a Rusty Nail, two. Doze. After a six-hour flight it will only be three hours later. Come to California, Dad. We'll swim in the pool, like you showed us at Jones Beach. *Glide, glide until just before you sink, then kick hard and glide.* Sit at the head of the table. Tell your grandchildren how you beat the world to its knees: *Cash in the bank, neither son in jail, a wife who took a long shot with me, and a new Bonneville.* You can bounce up, up from the diving board, and punch God in his Heaven-is-better-than-this-world face before you sink down past the full diaper moon, you're not my husband moon, gibberish moon, be her shadow all night in the 40-watt haze of that apartment in Queens moon.

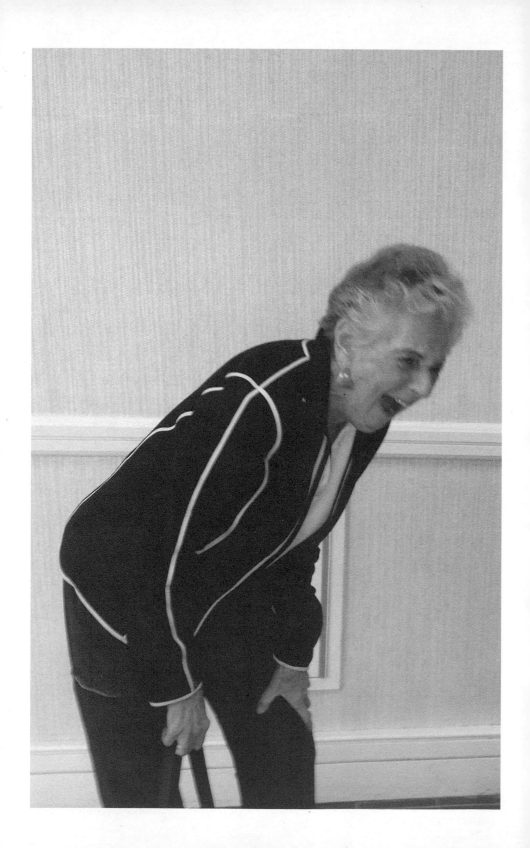

She Fools Me Every Time

When I discover my shoe
under her pillow and my credit cards
floating in the tub, I kiss her
for finding them.

Vile animal, she calls me
for taking her clothes
and washing them. I confess.

She changes my name: Peter to
Joe to Elizabeth. *Yes,* I answer.

We agree the neurologist stole
her driver's license when she wasn't looking
and that 2 a.m. is a *yummy time*
to split a tuna fish and ketchup sandwich.

When she soils herself and asks
if she smells, I take a big whiff, say, *No.*
Do I?

She leans her bony hands on my hips
and I turn for her to sniff
where only mothers are allowed to.

I wait to hear her say, *So fresh, Ben.*
Like flowers, Leo. I wait for her
to call me *Michael*. And I will turn

and we will see each other again.

The Wish

What if we get him a turtle? my mother asks
from behind her oxygen mask.

When she laughs, I do, too.

My father makes a fist
that looks like a claw, and shouts, *Fight harder!*
Mom nods, then coughs, sleeps more.

Five days later, I'm carrying
a tiny army helmet, half sunk
in a plastic oasis.

Dad jabs his rigid fingers
into the terrarium's sandy bottom,

picks the thing up.

Four flippers crawl against the air.
Four wet eyes lock in a stare-off.

I'm somewhere between
taking it back and a whiny, *But she said ...*

The little one slides its bald head left.
The big one, right.

I hear my mother laugh.

I do what she would: clean
the kitchen counter, make a place
by the window.

One of them nods like this could work.
One looks around at this strange world.

Watching the Golden Gate Bridge Disappear

Mom, I'm in San Francisco
   and the bridge
is being taken away.

The east tower
   is completely gone.
All morning

the pillars resisted the fog
   until they were exhausted.
Was it like that for you

when you didn't know how
   to make your famous
tuna the way I liked it

anymore
   and you kept calling me
the mean tailor? I needed

to take in your housedress.
   (You'd gotten so thin.)
The suspension cables

barely peek out now
   and the cars are creeping
into the invisible.

It's getting hard to remember
   how it was.
The locals tell me to just wait.

In a moment the whole bridge
   will return with the cars,
the boats, the bay, the sun.

What My Father Heard the Rabbi Say at My Mother's Funeral

And the Lord looked down upon this man and judged henceforth:
   the grocer will cut one steak.

For he shall be known all his numbered days as Bob
   and not Hubby, as she bestowed upon him for yea on 64 years
   and 10 months and 28 days, and not Bubby nor Sir Lancelot as she purred
   on blessed evenings, nor El Putzo when she cursed him in public.

So it was commanded: cleave this them to a him.

And let not Benny Goodman or Sinatra classic, nor corned beef sandwich
   from Ben's, nor hot streak at the tables, comfort this man
   as he had been comforted.

As leaves fall from winter trees, so shall her name, day by day, dwindle
   until forever vanished from the mail.

And lo—the sacred Social Security check shall be severely diminished.

And he shall suffer immeasurable woe.

When darkness descends, Bob shall wander the endless desert
   of his badly lit 600-square-foot apartment without staff, fiery cloud,
   shaggy slippers or crumpled tissues to follow all his sleepless nights.

And when dawn finally rises from the vast void, let not the Denny's waitress
   ever again divide a solitary Grand Slam and maketh two.

All those hallowed summer weeks in the Catskills: bridge and rummy, cubed
   fruit, dancing shoeless in the bungalow, shall be cast upon his memory as
   an everlasting plague.

[...]

And all the world shall pass him by in the way cars and trucks speed these days even in the slow lane, leaving only garbage in the wind on the Long Island Expressway.

So it was said and so it shall be done.

Then, sighed my father in his fortieth retelling in the 2 a.m. kitchen, *the Rabbi stopped talking, stepped down from the pulpit and we put her in the ground. And I don't care what he or God or even you thinks—I'm never taking her name off that mailbox.*

Spoiled

My father puts the milk carton
on the kitchen table. Declares, *She bought it—*
before. The two glasses tremble. I know worship

and gratitude. I know love taught by tender example
and backs of hands, thrift.
And that I am a spoiled child at sixty

because, until three days ago, both my parents
were alive, and as long as both your parents live, old
as you get, you are not an adult.

I do the math: she has been gone exactly seventy-three hours.
The stamp on the carton warns the milk expired five days ago.
The pulmonologist alerted me it was *a matter of hours.*
They were married two months shy of sixty-five years.

On special occasions, she'd put out fresh melon, cubed
and stuck with frilly toothpicks. He half fills both glasses
to make our toast, take our communion,

our poison. I know that the Bible says I owe. That
his word is law in this house. That in one night a wounded man
can wander a lifetime in a small apartment.

And how to fake swallow, then spit it out.

Nothing's as Hard as We Make It

Get out from under my feet, I tell her—
like she'd told me countless times. Go
have fun with the other dead moms.
She's not acclimating. The ladies look
nice, clean, I say. Go! She leans her weight
deeper. I give her a nudge, a *zetz,*
she'd call it—not so hard that she feels
I'm disappointed. Make me proud, I say.
Show the afterworld who my mother is.
She spits. Who made me an expert
in the afterworld? I open a bag of fresh
apples I thought of all morning—how
she picked them from the grocer's for me,
turned each slow, inspected every curve,
shading, dimples for soft spots—then all
afternoon I remembered how she washed
and dried, then shined them with her breath,
cut crisp slices. Take a piece mom—share.
This is Stella, this is Alice, and Tess.

Estelle and Bob

My father kneels at my mother's grave
to ask her permission to go on match.com.

He unfolds some pages it took him hours to print.
Eleanor enjoys bowling and the beach—the sand tickles her toes.
Sherri hopes to see London. Rachel is a twin. He crushes
the papers back into his jacket pocket. *Stupid.*

Other mourners speak to other graves. He returns
their only-we-know nod, slides a finger down
the first carved letter of the headstone, follows

them all, then the dates, wipes some nonexistent dirt.
Still looks new, he says. And he hopes she won't hate him—Benny
from the card game put him up to it. *Two dumb putzes.*

He pulls some short weeds, places three pebbles
on the craggy head of the stone, and sings
Happy Birthday, raising his voice at her name,
so everyone knows he's with her.

Dancing with My Father
at My Son's Wedding

There's no room on the floor, no place
he won't get bumped and I won't be able to stop his fall.
So we find a corner.
He's taken his hearing aids out—the band pounds
its assault. I take his hand, a former boxer's hand
with a father's thicker fingers.
He rests his wrist on my shoulder for me to lead.
I pull him closer, feel for his balance, find his eyes, unsure
if he sees mine. I nod once
and gently press him backwards, then to the side.
I study our black shoes, see him teaching me
to spit-shine, his brush punishing
the heels and toes like enemies. He wobbles.
I grab tight.
It was just a shuffle step, a fighter's feint.
He smirks, loves that I fell for it. I count out loud,
shouting over the music, as if he could hear,
as if this were about dancing.

First Date

Two old, two very old cars
in the supermarket parking lot,
side-by-side in the handicap zone.
This is how I see them, my father
and his new girlfriend. The 1926 Ford,
him, dented fenders, hubcap missing,
bald tires overlapping the blue line,
bumper almost scraping the scratched up
1930 Chevrolet, her. When he tells me
how they met I don't hear—it's already
in my head. Both cars backing out
of their spots at the same time. One
stopping short for the other to go. While
the other stops short for the other to go.
Then they both go, then stop, then go.
The screech of brakes. And he waits and
she waits until he hits his horn, *Come on
already!* And she gets nervous and moves
straight back into her spot to wait for him
to leave and he feels guilty and pulls up
beside her and waves for her to go first
but she just stares ahead, pretends
she doesn't see, hands gripped at ten
and two. So he shuts his engine and gets out,
locks the door, tugs on the handle to test
that it's locked so if he dies before he gets back
to it, no one should steal it, and walks around
and taps lightly, very lightly, on her window
though she pretends he's not there, can't hear
a thing, so he yells but tries not to make it an angry
yell, *I'm sorry my wife passed. I'm ...* He looks away.
This is where she rolls the window down close
to half, asks how many years they had together.

[...]

Sixty five. Almost. Missed by seven days. This is where she turns the key and shuts the engine. *And how many for you?* This is where she feels her foot ease off the brake.

My Mother's Freezer

Again, he climbs the three-step
step stool, pauses to catch his breath,
then folds his five-foot-four
inches over

then over and scooches
against the bumpy ice. Stabbing
back some with a screwdriver,

he tucks his bluish knees
and brown-socked feet, closes
himself in.

A sonogram of the freezer
would reveal a foil-covered cube
of potato kugel, *Hanukah 1973*

written in her hand, a Polaroid
she magic-markered on the back, *Catskills,
Summer 1957*, two scarves

her mother knitted, mummy-wrapped
in foggy cellophane and my dad
curled into a fetal position, the cold
freezing his tears.

This last part's not true.

Of course his tears don't freeze
in her freezer—which she'd swore, "not only
keeps everything as it was, it makes
them even younger"—they roll up

[...]

into his eyes, glaucoma and cataract-free
again, the years, months, days, clicking backwards
as he talks with her, shivering—touched
where she touched.

Celebrating His 92ⁿᵈ Birthday
the Year His Wife Dies

He goes to Ben's Deli
because the waitress doesn't ask how he is.
He takes most of the corned beef
from the sandwich, piles
it on the edge of the plate, makes
a thinner one, with enough left for two
nice ones at home.
The waitress packs his leftovers, extra
slices of rye and half sour pickles
in wax paper and two mustards in squat cups.
She never removes the other setting.
She lets him sit as long as he wants.

If I Say, The Butterfly Is Beautiful, Dad,

he'll say, it's a bug.

If I say it likes him,
he'll say, who needs friends?

If I say, once it was a caterpillar,
he'll say, next it'll be dead.

If I say, it's a symbol of change,
he'll inch his butt to the bench's edge,

rock back and forth, back and forth,
like the physical therapists taught him

to get momentum, to stand safely,
then after three settling breaths

he'll turn and start shuffling
towards the car.

If he's feeling steady enough, if
the breeze isn't too hard, he might

spread-wide those bony elbows
look back at me

and flap them.

A Daily Practice

After I write *Temporary* on each sticky note
and press them onto socks, silverware, bills,
my hair, I put one on each maple tree in the yard,
and notice I don't think of them as eternal
as much. All it takes is a single written word
on red, yellow, green tags to remind me
the car isn't mine. The house isn't mine. Snow,
money, flowers do that just being themselves
but I stick one on fear and another on hate,
pushing with all my weight so they stay. Dogs
are born with the knowledge, so no need. But
old people, even shrinking in hospice beds, yes.
Somehow they transform *Temporary* into *Still Here*.
Babies are so hard, I almost can't. When the pad
is empty, I wait for the glue to lose its grip and fight
the urge to blow or peel them off. Sometimes a wind
comes. And I stumble around, trying to catch them.

ABOUT THE RATTLE CHAPBOOK SERIES

The Rattle Chapbook Series publishes and distributes a chapbook to all of *Rattle*'s print subscribers along with each quarterly issue of the magazine. Most selections are made through the annual Rattle Chapbook Prize competition (deadline: January 15th). For more information, and to order other chapbooks from the series, visit our website.

www.R a t t l e.com/*chapbooks*